THE MEMOIRS OF SAPIENCE

Poetry Collection by Zuhair Irfan

Dedicated to the 3 philosophers
who've immensely shaped my mind:
Aristotle, Plato and Socrates

Contents

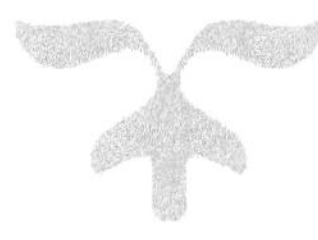

Part 1 – Life

Part 2 - Love

Introduction

Every Poet, I suppose, presumes that the readers of his or her work would benefit from reading it. The work ethic required to write a book, itself is an essential factor in the development of a book. My only aim for writing this book was to change the way people think. The way conventional wisdom operates in our minds, is tough to change. Conventional thoughts, are inherited to us by our ancestors, and it's usually embedded in our subconscious mind. My aim is not to eradicate those thoughts, which is impossible, but to replace them with better and more productive thoughts.

Many of us spontaneously anticipate how our friends and family would perceive our actions, without even doing something in the first place. We are people of free will, yet chained by the society's perceptions of us. We fail to create our own identity and rely on others to carve our character, and accept whatever we are told. Everyone fails at some point in their life, whether it be your career, relationships, financial decisions or your image, but those who stand up again would be the ones who would create their destiny.

I don't care whether you're dyslexic, black, or whether you have low IQ and EQ. I just want you to sincerely follow your passion despite of what everyone says. You need to step out of your comfort zone, and question the choices you make. Change your intuitive beliefs, and question your need for instant gratification.

In 1957 at the age of 80 Casals, a famous Cello Player, was the subject of a movie short, A Day in the Life of Pablo Casals. The movie's director Robert Snyder asked Casals, "why he continues to practice four and five hours a day." Casals answered: "Because I think I am making progress."

People are usually too afraid of what others think that they fail to improve. You need to improve your ability to carve your own identity, and understand errors of judgement and choice.

Much of the discussion in this book is about, how you can step out of your comfort zone and achieve whatever you want with the right amount of effort.

There are two parts in this book, Love and Life, both of which are commonly associated with each other. Love is a tool that is a source of both motivation and demotivation, it depends on what your significant other, parents, friends and family perceive of your actions. Whereas, life is an equally complex phenomenon as well. It helps you to create new habits constantly that improve you personally, financially, and socially.

The former helps you get started in the first place through unyielding support, whereas the latter helps you keep going on the projected trajectory. Love evolves like a sloth, whereas Life changes instantaneously.

It could happen that due to your circumstances you won't have, "Love", by which I mean unconditional support, but that shouldn't stop you in the process. Instead that should motivate you, when you're stuck in the obscure places in life. You can evolve love to coexist with your life, and by that I mean Self-love, which would have the most profound effect on your character.

For Life you'll need to have a steady pace, and be ready to change the realities anytime. Your habits, combined with a burning desire, as Napoleon Hill anticipated, would certainly prevent you from feeling any melancholy. You'll need to stay strong throughout the path, and you'll need the ability to differentiate between productivity and diversion, which would be the toughest.

No task is a day's work, it would take you a decade if not years to accomplish, and comprehending this would be the toughest when your mind is programmed for instant gratification. Everything can be achieved in the long run, despite of innumerable failures in the way. A quotation from Confucius might help, "When it is obvious that the goals can't be reached, don't adjust the goals, adjust the action steps".

Learning is a very tedious process, and even if you spend a century at it, still it won't be complete, but that shouldn't stop you from acquiring some of it.

Seeing the dream is important, but living through the dream and carving your own path is far more essential. Even if it means defying the conventional norms and values, you should go for it. The society has evolved significant in the past three decades and embracing change and being creative would help you go far.

You'll wonder why the Fortune 500 companies are successful? Why Israel has the best army? Why the USA has a strong hold on the global politics? All of it is due to innovation and creativity. Conforming to the old habits, won't help you differentiate from others, and you'll have plenty of competition.

Follow the Blue Ocean Strategy and explore new stuff, make yourself better each day, and you'll wonder what you can achieve.

Reading this book would help you realize where you're headed to, and each poem would help you develop a particularistic characteristic, in yourself which would help you either in 'Love' or 'Life'.

Some poems are filled with melancholy whereas many others are in a jubilant mood. It would help you to shed some tears, while simultaneously help you to head for the light, and your ultimate destination.

Part 1

Life

Taking Small Steps…

Don't be hard on yourselves
No one has an ace up their sleeves
You need to make your way to the top
And it only matters what you believe

Change your mindset, accept what's wrong
And you'll wonder what one can achieve
Do your best, neglect the criticism
It doesn't matter what someone else perceives

Get rid of fake friendships and carve your way
Reduce your burden and lower your eaves
Take tiny steps, in the realm of knowledge
And you'll wonder what one can retrieve

This World…

This world is a broken place
I never even liked it before
But there's nothing I can replace
There's nothing I can restore

Living in such a world is a disgrace
There's nothing I can do more
I don't know what I chase
I don't know what's life anymore

Everything here is a rat race
And there's a broken door
And it says it all, to my face
There's nothing here to explore

All my dreams were hard to erase
There was no sky, no wild roar
I was alone, there to unlace
And it was never like before

And yet my soul left me

With no intention to return

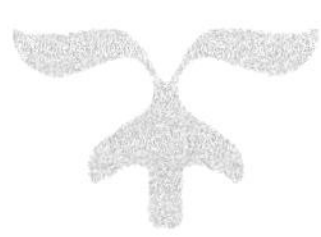

The Tests of life

The troubles brought by life are unpredictable
And you are usually saved by a miracle
The harder you try, the further you get
And the results then, become predictable

In these years of teenage you'll have great stress
And your anger would usually be irresistible
You'll spend a great deal of time on some things
And the results won't be explicable

Still you'll practice, for the sake of your future
Till your days become hospitable
And who knows how far you'll get
Till your days become miserable
I don't really understand happiness now
Nothing in the world is expectable
The one thing I struggled for, I couldn't get it
And these days would be unforgettable

I don't know what to do next
My conditions are not adjustable
But, still I'll stand up again for myself
So that my life becomes livable

Things are not working out for me now
But, most of the things are tractable
If I banish my regret, I'll stand up again
Or else my life for me, would be unforgivable

I know, I need to figure it out
And then I'll become formidable
But, it will take time to process all this
And these days won't be forgettable

You won’t anticipate what would come next

If you failed to account, the past

Capitalist System and Modern times

I'll need to fight for what's mine

But, that just won't be fine

My passion won't help me in the long run

I'll need a strategy, a perfect design

I know this world is meritocratic

And like a keyboard, I need to be chromatic

I need to find the perfect scale for myself

I'll find it so that I don't become dogmatic

I need to find a solution to this flawed system

Of whom everyone one is a victim

People judge us based on a piece of paper

Calling us unworthy, when we are full of wisdom

You won't see the world if you're perfect

And for me that would be a defect

Everyone deserves a chance to succeed

And this statement is a century old project

I've seen strong men crying because of it
I've seen many people with ambitions quit
The system exploits the people cruely
And labels them as a misfit

It's not the people's fault, the system is flawed
The motto is to get good grades, and get people to applaud
But, there is not a single drop of passion in it
And that's why the system is a fraud

Now I can't even say you to follow your dreams
Because employers want you to be machines
The school trains you for slavery
By managing your mind behind the scenes

You'll have a normal life until you know this
And this reality would then be hard to dismiss
I don't know whether you'll get ahead in life or not
But, you'll be the one who resists

Delayed Gratification

Lessons are necessary to grow
Failure is necessary to know
You'll have your burning desire
If your failures overflow

People fail to see the true you
And they don't even have a clue
They'll never know you
They'll never see the full view

Keep your goals to yourself
Be the ancient book on a bookshelf
People shouldn't hear you scream
Your passion should make them deaf

Keep looking forward to the light
It would keep you calm at night
You'd become a sage of wisdom
But, that day won't be tonight

You'll get ahead as time will pass

You won't break like a glass

Keep yourself together for some time

And the bad things would just surpass

Realize that you won’t make it today, but Each day you’ll be closer to your destination

Success Changes People .....

Life is just a long way

You're never meant to get ahead

And even if you do

People just get to your head

They feel uneasy around you

Because for them life is a dead end

They are never happy for you

Because jealousy is today's trend

Many people say they're happy

And trust me most people just pretend

You just need yourself to be strong

That's the only thing I recommend

The Old Realities

It's something about the sea
Or whether I feel safe ashore
There is always a way to escape
But I can't find it anymore

I am stuck in an island of thoughts
I am attracted to its core
I am waiting for that homerun
But, there's no way I can score

I am yet a droplet in the ocean
And there were many like me before
People love us for sometime
Until they can't remember us anymore

This is life, and its fairness I must say
There's no after and not much before
As you grow up you'll find out
The old realities aren't same anymore

The old realities will change like the sky

And the night won't let you see the day

Lessons in life ....

Life doesn't make any sense
And I always play on the defense
I stay away from some ruminations
So that it doesn't get any intense

I see people walk past me everyday
Draped in mystery, cloaked in pretence
I wonder what they'll do next in life
At someone's else expense

Everyone has their chances in life
Everyone has a commonsense
Failure is the beginning of a fruitful journey
So there's no reason for penitence

Continue, from where you lost a while ago
The lessons in the way would be immense
And if you fail again, remember me
It's a journey you'll need to recommence

Learning would never let you stop, stopping

Would never let you learn in the first place

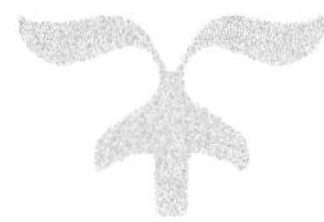

Finding Your Path

Don't be hard on yourselves
No one has an ace up their sleeves
You need to make your way to the top
And it only matters what you believe

Change your mindset, accept what's wrong
And you'll wonder what one can achieve
Do your best, neglect the criticism
It doesn't matter what someone else perceives

Get rid of fake friendships and carve your way
Reduce your burden and lower your eaves
Take tiny steps, in the realm of knowledge
And you'll wonder what one can retrieve

Regret – A Destructive Habit

Regret is a temporary stage
And it doesn't leave without a change
It touches the berm of the soul
And leaves people with rage

It is like living matter, it grows
Till it finally moves upstage
And then it gets much worse
Becoming a lion hard to cage

Control it when you can
Or its impact would be hard to gauge
We all make mistakes in life
And it's nothing strange

Mistakes are what make us human
And people can really change
Do what you can with the time you have
Regret is a temporary stage

Stressing on the past is not the solution, but The ability to adapt is what really matters

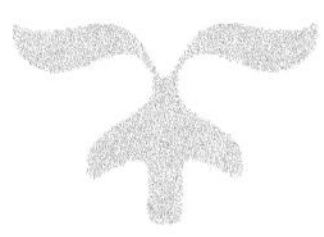

Disruption of Morality

I am no one to question them

But, our coming generations will breathe in the same air

No matter how modernized people get

You still need to be firm and debonair

Stay loyal to the principles of any religion you belong

The golden key is meditation and prayer

Strengthen your faith in a higher power

And then life will be square

The old ways were for the best

But today is a different world we share

It doesn't matter what others do

People like us, are today rare

Finding Yourself

Being lost is a state
And sometimes you don't want to be found
You want to be someone
You want to be crowned

You feel like the ocean tides
Always ready to rebound
You foresee these obstructions as limitless
Your success to the impound

But it simply isn't true
You can easily come unwound
Think of this situation as temporary
You're just, a puzzled soul around

Your Dreams and Yours Only

No one knows what you've been through
And you have a dream you want to pursue
I comprehend you profoundly
But, really no one needs the full view

Don't explain it to them, no one needs to know
Just strike them gradually out of the blue
Let them see the results of your efforts
And you'll see, the ones truly happy will be a few

Cut some slack, if you would
Scrutinize the whole crew
You'll find some naysayers on the way
Who might be hard to subdue
But, your efforts will pave the way
For your successes to accrue
And remember this voyage would be tough
But, it will surely sweeten up the brew

Don't forget what matters to you the most,

And that would be enough to keep you alive.

Escaping the rat race

It's important to put all the pieces together
But, the puzzle is tough to put in place
It's all a test destined for you
Designed for you to ace

Be fearless, and work diligently
And just keep a steady pace
You will get ahead in your life
From the lessons you embrace

And if you fail in the process
It's your steps you need to retrace
You'll find what you did wrong
The mystery would be unlaced

Everything happens for a reason
And you're stuck in a rat race

There are many people like you

Never think you're the only case

And if you succeed in the process

You'd be someone hard to encase

Find those who have a common purpose

And you'll see where they're headed to

Passion and Insecurities

Don't care what people think of you
Their words are explicitly not true
You can be short, ugly or dark
They don't know what you've been through

People take time to change opinions
And to specially to consider the full view
Don't let them bother you
You still have a life ready to construe

You need to find your passion
And you'll definitely learn something new
It could be music, dance, literature
Or the paintings in nursery you drew

Scrutinize your life closely
And some wisdom will accrue
It's your insecurities that hold you
And it's something you always knew

But, why me? Why do I have to tell this?

Because it's a process I've been through

Once you pass this exam you'll succeed

And people who go down this path are always a few

Do what you like, think what you want

Until it remains in the realm of morality

Life evolves at all times

Life evolves

At every stage

And it's not new

You are accustomed to the influx

Of changes

Of the people around you

Of the things around you

Too much that you forget

Why does this phenomenon occur?

Is it something with you or the others?

It's a feeling you conquer

By making excuses

You need to figure out

Let the devil stand out

You can evolve again

But this time

Without getting on a long train

Figure it out before it's too late

Make some changes and meditate

You can be arrogant, impatient, and lazy

You're not the only one

You're not crazy

Before getting on an emotional rollercoaster

Remember this phrase

" What brought you to these circumstances in the first place? "

Then all of it will make sense

And you'll figure out what you need to do

Without any pretense

You'll know

What's wrong and what's right

And definitely your future

Will turn out bright

You'll meet new people

Without the old faults

The old folks would also give you

Far less taunts

Your relationships would work again

Your life will kick start again

But, still life will evolve

And remember these are your problems

That no one else will solve

You're the one who limits yourself

You have no enemies, but you

Old memories

I feel there's still a chance
I believe I can do much more
But I can't go back to the old me
Those memories are frozen in a store

I turn with every passing tide
Unlike the shore
There's something else in this life
I wish to explore

But I don't seem to find it
It's like a room with no door
I see myself in a dark cave
Which I can't seem to ignore

Those memories are alive again
And they seem to fill the floor
I can't forget the past, and who I used to be
And it's killing me to the core

Memories are tough to hide

Always buried deep down in the soul

A Stage to Perform

You can either be quiet

Or provide everyone a stage to perform

It's your life, live the way you want, and

Don't let your heart in any way deform

There are people out there, who'd stop you

They'd give you blankets to feel warm

But, you don't need to accept sympathies

Or you'll be wandering naked in a storm

Pave your way with your own efforts

Leave the conventional wisdom, don't conform

It's your life, it's your own struggle

Don't provide everyone a stage to perform!

Struggles

Oppression is used by the weak
To inflict the ones
Who stay firm
It is a statement I stand with
It doesn't matter what you faced in the past
The future will be more tough
The standards of toughness will evolve
And you would be effected
Immeasurably by it
The stages of toughness would undergo
Dramatic transition
But, you'll be alone to face it all
At some times you'll have
Your friends and family
But, most of the times
You'll end up alone
No one can be similar to you
You're the one, the one of a kind

A Quantum entangled equation

You need to face all the struggles

To appreciate what you have now

To cherish the moments, you have

And that will be all what would

Keep you alive!

From the struggles of life itself

Your memories will pave the way

For the hardships to pass

And you'll wake up some day and remember

You wouldn't be where you are

Without all the efforts you did

And you'll see people around you

Who couldn't evolve

Who couldn't change their fate

Who were stuck in the past

And you'll be the one who survived

And that would be solely enough,

For you to spend,

What would be left of your life

No one can understand you

It's you who needs to understand yourself

A Rare Jigsaw Puzzle

People are very different than you
And you're a rare piece
You need to fit in a puzzle
But you can't find the other piece
It's a mismatch
You'll have for a long time
And you'll struggle to find
Others like you
But you'll still be stuck in time
And rejecting others,
Would limit your progress
And people
Who you thought were family
Would give you the most stress
Some might help in the journey
Some might prevent you to progress
You'll need to differentiate between
Friends and foes

But, still you'll always be

Better on your own

Keep things to yourself

Don't ask for validation

Don't let them kill your dreams

Don't let them feel your emotions

Or else you'll be vulnerable

For them to pry on

Be the true you

And don't let them have a clue

You'll find the other pieces

You'll have your own cue

You'll do a break on the table of life

And you'll wait for things

To turn out to be true

You'll find your destiny

You'll find something new

And then life

Won't be the same as before

I'll find my part on the scroll, and you find yours

But, changes in destiny is what everyone will ignore

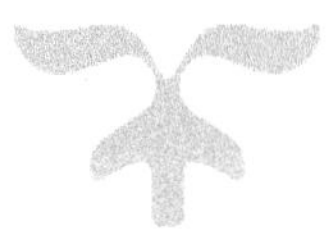

Procrastination

The old days have gone
My whole life has been redrawn
My realities have changed
I have people to mourn

I have new theories about the world
And the truth is a bit curled
There's always a lie beneath the truth
Making the reality seem blurred

I have seen so much so early
And I have a lot, I ought to worry about
My aspirations have always been noble
And certainly there's no doubt

I have a goal in my mind
With an action plan well defined

I know what I'll need to execute
Everything is now intertwined

Still I am waiting, for my moment
And its procrastination I can't debate
I'm lost in the midst of this chaos
And it's a situation no one can relate

I need to have a duel with myself
Like in the old days they did
And it's all for the better, I know
It's a gamble, but I'll place my bid

I'll be a different man

I am a Man

I can't break down into tears

I wish to withhold my emotions

I want to wait

For serenity to engulf me

I'll wait

For the good days

To come

I know time will pass

As conventional wisdom has held

But, it's really me

Who needs help

I know I've to focus on the little things

That matter

The intricate details

In a painting

And only then I'll realize

The beauty within my gloominess

Time will only pass then

If I face my fears

Deal with my insecurities

And prove my adversaries wrong

Only then I'll be happy

Still, for that I'll need some motivation

To kick in

But, what greater motivation is there

Than being my ideal self

That I always wanted

I'll let myself soak in these ideas

And then I'll sort myself

For after that I'll be a different man

Losing Everything

Wait till you drown

In your own arrogance

Wait till you finally lose

Your elegance

It will be the time, people will

Finally realize

You're not worthy

Of your own inheritance

People will look at you differently

You'll end up fearing the unknown

And the reason won't be arbitrary

All along it would be you!

The destroyer of yourself

It is not Allah, not Jesus, not Shiva

That destroys you

It's yourself that does all the damage

And you tend to blame your destiny

For being so frivolous

Why?

The solution of destruction

Has always been creation

No matter what you've lost

On the outside

Solitude always begins inside

You'll need to sort yourself out

To finally prevent all the destruction

You've begin

And after that you'll find

The so-called, "Self Love"

And then things won't

Be the same again

After you give your destiny

Your life

Your mindset

A stupendous spin

Gen Z and elderly

Your elders are the ones

Who struggled

To give you a better future

And you're the one playing games

On a computer

All those efforts have ended in vain

You had a legacy you couldn't maintain

They fought battles for you to survive

For you to be alive

They were the ones who gave up

Their time for you

And all this time you had no clue

And you're placing them in nursing homes

And then what?

Who knows?

Your role was to give them time

Get there blessing for the time ahead

But, you thought of yourself

And you went in a pit hole
A dead end
You could get great wisdom from them
But, this is a statement
You highly condemn
You considered them a burden
And the truth was always behind a curtain
You couldn't reach for it
Even if you tried to
You had a perception of them
Which was something new
You considered them irrelevant
To your circumstances
But, what truly happened over time
Was that, standards of efforts evolved?
But, that is something you won't understand
And when the coming generations
Would do the same
You'll get the stress which you won't withstand
And then you would feel the pain

You will be filled with sorrow, which
You won't be able to contain,
Life will give you a lesson! too late
And you'll be left in a miserable state
But you still have time to change
There are a couple of values and norms
You'll need to replace
And after that you'll be fine
As your ancestors were
And you'll be the son and daughter
Your parents were

Time

You need to step up to the plate

Or else you would be late

Time is extremely important for you

And this thought is definitely innate

You pretend to value time

And I just don't want to get in a debate

Just know this when you waste time

That you'll need to recreate

Let yourself be the one

The one who can dictate

Forget what your mind says

There are various possibilities it can create

It can give you doses of false consciousness

Which can make it hard for you negotiate

But, it's your life and your terms

And it's never too late

Part 2

Love

When you left!

You left me when I had nothing
I don't remember you anymore
You left me alone in the dead sea
And my life was never like before

You said it straight to my face
"We can't be together anymore"
After that night my life changed
I was a broken relic, hard to restore

Life made me succumb to my wounds
And there was nothing for me ashore
I let myself weep until all the pain left
And after that I wasn't myself anymore

All could do ….

I never heard back from you
I guess our love was never true
I was entitled to a gruesome fate
And to which no one could relate

In life we never get the full view
And some things are too good to be true
Feelings are always hard to translate
And we are usually too impatient to wait

I guess it was never my dream to pursue
The chosen path was for the few
All I could do was to recreate
Just to be patient and wait

Processing memories

You left me before I could find you
You were an old film; I couldn't unwind you
I was left broken in tears
My heart had a million spears

The sun shined brightly in my eyes
As if it wanted me to rise
But what sense did it make
All I wanted was a break

Everything was too hard to process
And it did not make any sense
This was not what life was meant to be
There was none that I could foresee

.

Just another day!

It all happened again
There was no one I could blame
All my efforts ended in vain
I guess life is just an old train

For me life's just a prick
It's just another old trick
It stands at the corner to test me
And falls on my head like a brick

I could just wait for the sun to shine
And I could then end up just being fine
But what good would it do me
So it's an offer I would humbly decline

There was no one I could blame
There was no love I could reclaim
I was alone in my own world
With a broken heart yet to tame

Who would help me with my mistake?

Who would help me take a break?

I forgot it was December again

And I had my own reasons to stay awake

Love is a cure for the broken

For me it's a dead man's slogan

It's something I've chosen to embrace

It's something I've left in the wild to unlace

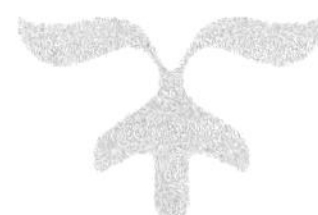

Leaving you!

There was nothing much I could do
And whatever I said wasn't true
I loved you before
But now you are something new

I know there are some hard feelings
All my words have dual meanings
But this is the world where we live
There is no one to back you for healings

I told you I wasn't going to return
And that was something hard to learn
I know you had tears in your eyes
But that's just life, it strikes at every turn

I didn't want to leave you at all
But this world is just so small
You thought I wouldn't know about it
But you know I couldn't avoid the fall

I just had to go with the flow
And I needed to grow
If I couldn't trust you anymore
Then it was time for you to go

It was hard for me to leave
Because I was the one to grieve
I didn't know things would end so quick
But that was just my belief

Every day is a new test!

Let's slow down and talk something else
I know feelings are not easy to express
Some people are not just ready to hear
And that's part of their progress

I know people who were on the defense
And they are known for taking little steps
There were people also on the offence
And those guys were a bit too intense

The way for you is to figure out the best
Because life is just a science project
You never know what gets in your way
Every day is a new test

Fire!

My heart was filled with fire

But not with a roaring desire

The signal was at amber

For which I had no answer

I had everything before

Everything was fine before

But now

None was left

Everything was stolen

Everything was kept

Despite of asking everyone in my way

The only way left for me was to pray

I saw something

I wasn't meant to see

I loved a liar

And yet there was she

I saw it in her eyes

When we first met

And that was something

I could never forget

I thought my instincts could be wrong

And that was my biggest mistake all along

I was left with a choice to make

All of it was for my own sake

I was left with a fragmented heart

And a life hard to restart

All I could do was to wait

For things to turn out great.

An amiable young man ….

Love is like faucet
And I am an amiable young man
You seem to fit my puzzle, the pieces
While no one else can

You are the key to the locks of life
And you make me gullible enough to believe it
Even when I am away
You make sure that I'll never quit

What lays ahead of time no one knows
But, I am sure I'll find you somewhere
I take solace in my quest of love
Which is the only thing now, I seem to care

"Leaving someone is hard"

It's true what everyone says
"Leaving someone is hard"
You remember all those moments
All of which you regard

It feels as if life is tormenting me
And yet you played a big part
It doesn't feel right to be with you
Our differences have grown apart

I feel as if I could be wrong
And the result of it could be a bit intense
But, from the very start to the indefinite end
Nothing in our relationship makes any sense

When we first met

It all happened instantly
When I looked into your eyes
I definitely knew I needed to reply
But at that time all the confidence dries

Didn't know you came to say goodbye
Was it my mistake or it's just that time flies?
At that time all I could do was to comply
And then it was broken vows and watery eyes

Losing someone close

A forest full of mahogany
A tree full of thorns
I see some motion in the sky
The clouds also mourn

They know me better than myself
They know I lost
But, truly it was our paths
That never really crossed

I felt the rage in my soul
I couldn't foresee any of this
I was left alone, yet banished
In the scorching abyss

I saw what losing in life really meant
And I couldn't change my fate
My feelings were inscribed in Sumerian
The symbols were hard to translate

Memories are tough to recall

Especially, when they are bad

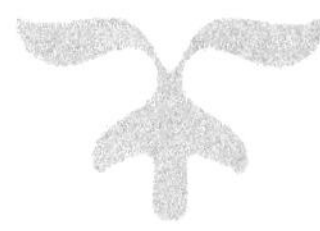

Finding a soulmate

You would never know how I felt
It's a situation hard to comprehend
My luck was tried several times
And I couldn't even pretend

My face revealed the truth
And those who know me I can't even lie
I am dreamer, in this cruel world
An eagle who cannot fly

I have tried many times to embark,
On the quest of love
But I seem to ignore my surroundings,
And all that lies above

I want to try again, try to win
And this time I'll find someone
It's just a matter of time
Before I'll find the one

Lead everyone who falls in your way

Helping people won't prevent you from success

You'll find everyone you want along that path

And it's truly a journey that won't make you regress

Birds and Humans

The birds chirping in the wild
Their rhythm perfectly styled
They express themselves effectively
By having the tune well defined

Their emotions flowing through cypresses
Their feeling is mutual and combined
They are not like humans
Static emotions, already ascribed

They are free, unchained like us
And their interests coincide
And what if we were like them?
It would be a matter of pride

But, unfortunately we have evolved
Followed a strategy to divide
And the day we stop it mutually
Our interests would be aligned

Some memories are too rough to tell, and

It's for the best that they should be forgotten

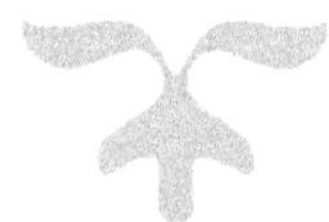

Love and fate

We could be together
Or we could end up alone
It depends on us entirely
The results would be unknown

We might grow to like each other
Or we can end up on our own
It all depends on our likes and dislikes
There is no proper way shown

As conventional wisdom has held
The light from above would be shown
It all depends on our fate
The only thing which we can't disown

Devout Followers

Leading a way is tough

And especially when

You have a burden to carry

No one will even know

What it feels like?

People are followers of a light

And you are the one in control

You might be afraid to lead

But, you're the only one to lead

People need a direction

A diversion from everyday's routine

And what you'll provide them with

Would be more than

Any diversion could ever be

You know the ways of this world

And you still keep it hidden

What good will your disciples be?

Knowledge should be amended with time

And applied to every phenomenon

You'll know it sooner than others

What good would the meta-narratives be?

Your job is to sell dreams

To the misfortunate

Help them differentiate between

Friends and foes

But what good will your leadership be

If you have been risk averse?

Don't promote rigidity

Let some love spread in the air

And you'll find the people with time

The ones who really care

Time for the Call!

It will take time before you meet

The one who would be

From your dreams

There's a difference between

Reality and illusion

It will take time for you to understand

The gravity of the situation and

Its full extent

But that won't be a problem at all

You'll definitely know

When it's time for the call

Take action with a steady pace

And your steps would be hard to trace

No one would ever know you fell in love

No one would ever catch you in the maze

You’d be someone they couldn’t anticipate

And for them

You won’t be a matter of debate

It just depends on when you realize

That it's your life, in your hands

And it's not a community project

For everyone to participate

The One!

I know you're the one
Your eyes describe you well
Your shyness explains everything
All that you wouldn't dare to tell

I suppose I should tell you
About how I feel
And after that my emotions
Won't be cascading on a wheel

But, what if doesn't turn out as I want
I'd then be stuck in the past
Remembering all the moments,
All the time you surpassed

I'd be broken to the core
It would be a damage hard to restore
But, I'll find a way as I always did
I know I'm an old bookstore

It's all my imagination
It's all just stuck in my mind
I guess it's my past experiences
That I dare not to rewind

I should try my luck this time as well
And maybe I'll succeed
It's one golden shot that I'm looking for
And that's what I really need

I know I'm procrastinating
Which I really shouldn't do
If I get my chance and succeed
I'd be a new person indeed

Foretelling the ancient scrolls

Meeting new people everyday
Changing presumptions every day
I've met people who had the drive
To change their realities everyday

But I can't forge that into me
Everyone is unique
And it doesn't matter usually
When life itself appears oblique

Life will unseal the greatest wonders
You'll find someone you're meant to be with
And then your story will be remembered
Unlike Ero, Athena or any of the Greek myth
You'll be with the love of your life
All your dreams would come true
And after that you won't be the same
You'd become a far better version of you

You should better find your destiny

And you'll wonder what would unleash?

Judging People!

Incorporated by laws
Marriage has its own flaws
Being single is never the aim
But, there can be a right cause

Don't judge people externally
There are emotions, that people suppress
You'd never know what one's been through
And it will be hard for you to process

But, over time you'll get the gist of it
And you'll understand people truly
You'll give people chances
You'll review them profusely

You'll learn to love your surroundings
And will be contented with all you have
You'll be a new lover, one of a kind
And you'll care for all you have

Don't trust what you see

Your intuition can be wrong as well

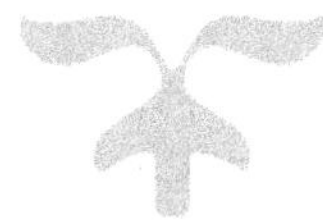

Moving the clock!

It can be hard to express
The emotions attached to someone
It can be spoken out loud
Or kept in dark
Still time will pass
Forgetting you in the way
And the moments
Would freeze in time
And you'll be nothing
But an atomic clock
Drifting through time
Won't help save you
It would instead make it worse
But, there is still something
You can do
Forget the past
Cherish the moments you have
Express yourself, whenever
You have your golden pass

It would save you
From an emotional rollercoaster
And it would make the clock
To move on!
You'll live like there's no tomorrow
And you'll improvise your past
Which would make you better
Much better than the past
You'll procreate yourself
With the knowledge you possess
And then there would be no possible reason
For you to stress
You'll have a nice future
You'll have plenty of success
It's a lesson you need to spread
And it's a nice speech to address
But, remember all of it is a reboot button
In your mind
Which you need to press
And then the clock would
Move on!

Things are not as easy as they seem, and
To succeed you'll need a higher self esteem

Love, life and efforts!

Struggle while you can

Hustle while you can

No one will ever tell you

The extent of "what you can?"

It's a unique path for you

And you're the only one who can

Really get to know the probable events

That would inflict your life

It's a mixture of possibilities and certainty

Which you'll explore on the way

Whether it's love or life

Everything is possible

With a consistent effort

And a long term mindset

You'll be ready for the sail

You'd face the wind

Avoid the rocks

And you won't sink in the antarctic even

It all depends on your preparation

That would ensure

That you're bound to succeed

Even if you have to jump in the sea

To merely survive

Then do it!

And then you'll rise up again even higher

And that consistent effort would make

You reach to the top

And then you'll learn

The principle of adversity

Which would be by far

The most important thing

You can possess

The Close Ones

You are someone

Whom I can talk with

All the time

And I won't really

Have to spend a dime

There's just so much similarity in us

And there's so much left

Still to discuss

I feel like I'll be with you

For eternity

And we'll make the perfect

Confraternity

Our friendship would continue

Till the end of time

And the memories

We'd make in the way

Would be sublime

I gaze upon the future sometimes

And I wonder if our friendship

Would remain the same?

But, I know

We'll remember the past

The memories

The young versions of us

Which would be cast in a frame

We would have responsibilities

In our life

Later on

But. it would definitely be our past

That we would proudly acclaim

My Peace

You make me
Feel important
Feel valued
Feel indispensable
But, it isn't really true
All that you think of me
For I am really
A different man
To you, I appear timid
But, my heart only knows
All the memories
I have kept a lid on
I feel like
I need to be diligent
I need to make some sacrifices
I need to shift my perspective
But, all I know
Is that my goals would remain the same
It's only the journey that'll change

I don't recognize my potential yet

I don't know where I am headed to

But, still I know one thing for sure

You'll be my beloved

My comrade

The epitome of my strength

I know I won't break again

I am willing to build a future

A future of my dreams

But, I know for sure

My milestones would only be reached

If we can be together

On this journey of life

We'll have our moments

We'll live a great life

Also success won't matter,

More than the journey would

And after that I'll die a happy man

Reliving my memories

And remembering how

It all began

I'm not the ideal person you want

For I am a man dwelled in past

My Aspirations

There are many reasons I adore you
And I know I was a different person before you
Now I pay attention to every intricate detail
Scrupulousness has begun, I assure you
I have changed for the better I know
I have been intermittent in my highs and lows
But, things have been quiet for a while
And I'm still going with the flow
I know I'll be better off in the end
"A man on whom everyone could depend"
I'm a complex person to figure out
Yet alone to befriend
But, my dawn will come soon to rise
My adversaries would be full of surprise
I'll triumph over anyone who comes in my way
I'll be the sole victor to arise

I know I am the one

And there are no limits to what I'll become

Conclusion

I hope this book benefits to those who read.
I have given my whole heart to this book.

With poetry, there are no limits for a Poet
The rich tapestry of emotions one can tap into

Is really beyond words, beyond anything
The knowledge, the lessons one can find

Are resourceful, in finding one's destiny
No one can debate one's purpose in life

It's always better for one especially
To figure it out, themselves

Life can give us tortures, reasons to lament
But, in the end it's always us

The one who needs to stand up
And face whatever lies beyond.........

www.ingramcontent.com/pod-product-compliance
Lightning Source LLC
LaVergne TN
LVHW050602160826
845677LV00011B/2432